GOLF *Is a Four-Letter Word*

G O L

THE INTIMATE CONFESSIONS OF A

With Tee-to-Green Illustrations by

F
Is a Four-Letter Word

HOOKED SLICER BY *Richard Armour*

Leo Hershfield

 Lyons & Burford, Publishers

Printed in the United States of America

10 9 8 7 6 5 4 3 2 1

Library of Congress Cataloging-in-Publication Data

Armour, Richard Willard, 1906–
Golf is a four-letter word : the intimate confessions of a hooked
slicer / by Richard Armour ; with tee-to-green illustrations by Leo
Hershfield.
p. cm.
Originally published: New York : McGraw-Hill, 1962. With new
introd.
ISBN 1-55821-222-1
1. Golf—Anecdotes. I. Title. II. Title: Golf is a 4-letter
word.
GV967.A7 1993
796.352'0207—dc20   92-45798
                                                     CIP

Introduction

You know how it is when you take an irrational dislike to someone. The malicious side of your nature seizes the opportunity, and rationality is suspended to pile on the hatred. Pretty soon some inoffensive soul who has never done you an atom of harm has grown into a loathsome ogre. Probably you don't know how it is, come to think of it, because if you do have a malicious side to your nature, you doubtless have it under tight control. Not me, though. I have to confess that there was a time when I abhorred the very name Richard Armour.

It happened like this. I was a young man just starting out on a career as a golf writer. A publisher had commissioned my first book and I positively hugged myself with smug satisfaction because I had thought of the perfect title. Then my world collapsed. In a second-hand bookshop I saw my title: "Golf is a Four Letter Word." How dare somebody steal my brainwave? And who the hell was Richard Armour? Could he be the son of Tommy Armour? Very likely. If so, he would undoubtedly be a better golfer than me, another good reason to hate his guts. I bought the book and it became the first volume in a golf library that was to grow like a triffid and, in time, compress my family into one small living room.

I was well aware that P.G. Wodehouse's publisher had asked him for a substitute title because several authors had already chosen "Summer Lightning." Wodehouse declined to make any change and wrote a witty introduction to his book expressing the fond hope that it might perhaps make the top-ten among books called "Summer Lightning." Such a course of action was not open to me, I felt. How could a young author hope to survive a charge of plagiarism? I made do with "The Game With A Hole In It," hoping I might pick up a few extra sales among the dimmer denizens of the soft-porn market. In time I settled down to read *Golf Is A Four-Letter Word* and, like everyone else, I was enchanted. Any animosity remaining in my system melted away. I began to like Richard Armour, whoever he might be. I made a note to watch out for anything else he might write. And then something happened to endear him to me even more. The golf-book collecting virus spread to epidemic proportions and my first edition of *Golf Is A Four Letter Word* increased in value a hundredfold from the modest sixpence I had paid. And it continues to go up. It seems I made a pretty shrewd investment when I backed my good pal Richard Armour. Bully for him. And bully for you for buying this book. I can't promise it will make you rich in worldly wealth, but you have acquired literary riches in ample measure.

—Peter Dobereiner

January, 1993

Chapter
One

I was, in a manner of speaking, seduced on our front lawn, when I was about fifteen, and my mother and father were sitting on the porch, watching. My seducer was a tall, slender youth, about a year older than I, who had a kind of worldliness about him that made him seem at least eighteen. My parents were impressed by his politeness and his good taste in clothes and were forever holding him up to me as an example.

"Notice how Gordon always jumps up when older people come into the room," my mother frequently told me, making one of her invidious comparisons. "You never see him chewing gum in public. And his clothes are always so neat and new-looking."

"Yes, Gordon's a fine boy," my father chimed in, Gordon being one of the few subjects on which he and my mother agreed. "You," he said to me, "could learn a few things from him." (As it turned out, I did.)

My parents were unaware that Gordon was a snake in the grass (or on the lawn, which I am coming to in a minute). If he jumped up when older people came into the room, it was only because he was taken by surprise while doing something he shouldn't have been doing, such as rolling a cigarette out of corn silk and tissue paper. As for not chewing gum in public, he was simply quicker than most of us at shifting a wad to a place under his upper lip, from which it would almost never drop down while he was polishing the apple with my parents. And those neat, new-looking clothes? It happened that his father owned a clothing store, and Gordon wore things a couple of months and then his father sold them for new. That was why he was so careful not to get them stained or ripped.

Anyhow, my father and mother just sat there on the front porch, rocking and smiling, the day Gordon came over and did me in.

It was a pleasant spring day back in 1921, and I remember it well, especially during my recurring nightmares. Gordon looked as neat and well-mannered and innocent as ever when he sauntered up the walk to our house.

"Good afternoon, Mrs. Armour," he said to my mother, doffing his cap and bowing slightly. "Good afternoon, sir," he said to my father. "Hello," he said to me.

"Hi," I said back, short and to the point. Then, noticing he was carrying something that looked like a cane, "Hurt yourself?"

"Of course not," he said. "I just wanted to know if I could practice on your lawn. We don't have any sprinklers."

"Practice what?" I asked. "And what do you need sprinklers for?"

"It's not the sprinklers I want," he said, "it's the sprinkler holes. Look."

While speaking, he had reached into his pocket and brought

out three white balls. These he placed in a row near one of the sprinkler holes. Then, bending over and swinging the head of what I had thought a cane, he hit the three balls, one after another, in the direction of a sprinkler hole about ten feet away. One of the balls went into the hole, and he looked pleased.

"How do you like that?" he asked, as if he had done something pretty important.

Then he picked up the three balls, lined them up again, and one after the other hit them toward the next sprinkler hole. None of them went into the hole this time, but one stopped only a few inches away and he seemed satisfied.

"Want to try?" Gordon asked, holding out the stick. It was about three feet long, with a piece of metal at one end.

"Sure," I said. It seemed kind of silly, but I had nothing better to do, and my mother and father were looking approvingly from the porch, glad to have me associating with someone like Gordon.

"Try to get as close as you can to that sprinkler hole," Gordon said, pointing at a hole halfway across the lawn, near the sidewalk. "Play the ball off your left heel, bring the club-head straight back, using mostly wrists, and follow through with a pendulum motion. There's a slight roll off to the right, and the green is slow, since it looks as if you haven't mowed your lawn for a week. Play a little to the left and remember, 'Never up, never in.' Just get as close as you can and don't be discouraged; it takes a lot of practice."

I wasn't listening much to Gordon, and didn't understand what he was talking about, anyhow. He had got down about to "don't be discouraged" when I gave the ball a jab with the metal end of the stick. The ball rolled across the lawn and

5

dropped into the sprinkler hole, where it nestled on top of the sprinkler inside.

"Well, there it is," I said. It had been ridiculously easy. "Shall I hit another one in?"

"Beginner's luck," Gordon said. "You did everything wrong—lifted your head, dipped your right shoulder, lunged at the ball, didn't follow through. Try it again, but you'll never get another in with a stance like that."

I moved over by the second ball and poked at it the way I had before. It rolled across the lawn and fell into the sprinkler hole just like the first one.

"Shall I do it again?" I asked.

"No," said Gordon, who took the stick away from me and picked up the three balls, "never mind." Then, after a pause, "I don't feel like playing golf today."

"Oh," I said, "this is golf?"

"This is putting. It's part of the game, but there's a lot more to it."

As I look back on it, this was a turning point in my life. Had Gordon put those balls in his pocket and headed for home, things might have been very different. But Gordon was, I am convinced, an instrument of the Devil, put on earth to bring sorrow and tribulation to innocents like me, and to turn them into liars and cheats and boasters and wife-deserters.

"Tell you what I'll do," he said, setting the three balls down on the lawn, in a row, "if you can get one of these balls into that sprinkler hole from here, I'll give you a dime. If you can get two in, I'll give you a quarter." I had never known Gordon to risk such sums of money before. I hated to take advantage of him, but just at the moment I could make good use of a dime, being out of chewing gum. I could see myself going on a Juicy Fruit jag, three sticks at once.

"You're on," I said, taking the stick from him and bending over the ball as before. Then I gave the ball a jab and watched it roll across the lawn about two feet, leaving me eight feet short of the sprinkler hole.

"Guess I hit that one too easy," I said apologetically. I still had two balls left, and could get my quarter all right by knocking them in.

"Try another," Gordon said. He seemed a little more relaxed.

"I'll hit this one a little harder," I promised, and gave the ball a pretty good poke. It went across the lawn nicely this time, and across the sidewalk and into the street, where it rolled along the gutter.

"One more," Gordon said. He was the old Gordon now, confident and cocky, running his thumb and forefinger down his trousers to freshen up the crease.

No chance for the quarter, but there was still a dime at stake. I settled over the ball carefully, and tried to remember some of the instructions Gordon had given me when I wasn't listening. At least I wouldn't hit it too easy or too hard.

I struck the ball just about right, and it went rolling across the lawn. It would have dropped into the sprinkler hole if I had been facing around a little more. As it was, it ended up about five feet to the left.

"Not so easy, is it?" Gordon said, picking up the balls and reaching for the stick.

"Let me try it just three more times," I begged. "I know I can do it again."

"All right," Gordon said, "but you'll have to pay me a dime for every time you miss, or three misses for a quarter." Gordon, I always thought, had a good business head on him, and if I had been bigger, I'd have knocked it off.

For half an hour I tried to hit the ball so it would roll across the lawn and fall into a sprinkler hole. But something happened every time: I hit the ball too easy or too hard or to the right or to the left. Gordon kept track on the back of an envelope.

"How much is it now?" I kept asking, and he kept telling me, gladly. When he got up to two dollars and a quarter, I

8

quit, having used up my allowance for nine weeks. I could see I was going to be a long time chewing spruce gum, scraped off the Fergusons' tree, before I ever got back to Juicy Fruit.

But after Gordon left, with his three balls and the stick and forty-five cents and my I.O.U. for a dollar eighty, I kept remembering how I had put the ball into the sprinkler hole two times in a row, and I knew I could do it again.

The next Sunday I went out to the Mountain Meadows Country Club, of which Gordon's father was a member, and carried a man's clubs (they weren't sticks, I discovered, they were clubs, used for beating up innocent golf balls) while he played around the course, swearing and lying when he should have been in church.

One Sunday a few weeks later, I went back to the Mountain Meadows Country Club, which by this time I had persuaded my father to join because it would help his business, and carried his clubs while he played Gordon's father. Gordon's father won every hole from my father, at twenty-five cents a hole, and took four dollars and a half from him, and my father, who couldn't see how this was helping his business, quit playing golf right then and gave me his bag of clubs.

The following Sunday I played my first game of golf at Mountain Meadows with Gordon, and he won every hole and took ninety cents from me, playing for five cents a hole. But I had no one in the family to give my bag of clubs to, being an only child, and besides my father said I had talked him into joining the Mountain Meadows Country Club and somebody had to get his money's worth out of the membership fee and the dues. However, I gave up playing for such high stakes and eventually gave up playing with Gordon when I found a boy two years younger than I who was musclebound and had no sense of distance. We had some close games together, and I would sometimes take a hole from him, with nine strokes to his ten.

By this time, as you can see, I had the golf habit, and all because of what Gordon did to me out on our front lawn. Our yard was no Eden, but I know how Eve felt when the Serpent got through with her.

Chapter
Two

It did not occur to me at the time, but I now see why Gordon led me down the primrose path to the first tee. His father, as I have said, was the owner of a clothing store. What I have not said is that it was called The Toggery, and it specialized in sports togs, on which there was apparently a higher mark-up than on business suits.

My father, still embittered from having lost that four dollars and a half to Gordon's father and from having bought a complete golf outfit which he never wore again, explained the high price of sports togs to me.

"Fashions change every season," he said, "and a merchant has to raise prices to make up for the out-of-style clothing he sells the next year at a reduction." Then my father, who enjoyed a good pun, or even a fair one, as long as it was his own, said, "Every tog has its day, you know." As soon as he said it I could tell, from the length of time he laughed, that this was one we would be hearing again.

Anyhow, I'm convinced that Gordon, who worked in The Toggery after school and Saturdays, had an outside job something like that of a narcotics pusher. The more people he could get to play golf, the more business his father would do with sports togs, and I am sure Gordon got a commission.

"Here's a list, Gordon," I can imagine his father's saying. "See how many you can get hooked this week." And Gordon would be off with his three balls and his putter, tracking down some sucker with sprinkler holes in his front lawn.

Gordon's father was a Director of the Mountain Meadows Country Club, which was just getting started and not doing any too well. But I doubt that loyalty to the Club completely explained his keeping a stack of membership blanks alongside the cash register. There was probably a going rate of about ten dollars a head on any new members who could be rounded up.

They got us for the works: membership in the Club, a complete outfit for my father, and, a short time afterward, a complete outfit for me. My father's clubs were a little heavy, but I could use them, by choking down on the handles about six inches, like a batter getting ready to bunt. His golf togs, however, were no go.

"You can take them in a little, can't you?" my father asked my mother hopefully. He was a little naive about tailoring, never having been able to thread a needle, and failed to appreciate the difficulties involved in reducing a 42-inch waist to a 28. Alterations, my mother insisted, were out of the question. And there was no postponing the membership fee twenty or thirty years, until I had developed a paunch like my father's.

So I went to The Toggery to get fitted out. My mother and father went with me, to see that Gordon's father didn't sell me something a couple of sizes too large, lacking anything in my subnormal size. Alone, how was I to know that Gordon's father, instead of smoothing the cloth in back, was holding

it in his fist, doubled over, and pulling? With my mother standing in front and my father in back, there could be no monkey business. Besides, my father always liked to feel the cloth between his thumb and forefinger, screwing up his face and making clucking noises with his tongue.

"Mmm," he would say after feeling the cloth very carefully, or "Well," or something equally discerning, while Gordon's father looked respectful and concerned, as if in the presence of an international expert on textiles.

This time, of course, I was not buying a whole suit, but just a golf outfit, consisting of plus fours, a sweater, socks, and rubber-soled shoes. The most important item was the plus fours, a kind of knickers that had to hang exactly right if they were to make the wearer look like Gene Sarazen or Walter Hagen and not like a boy who had put on his mother's bloomers by mistake.

"Let's try these for size," Gordon's father said, taking a

green-and-white pair from the shelf and heading me toward a corner of the stock room, partitioned off by a blanket hanging from a curtain rod. There is hardly any use knocking on a blanket to see whether a place is occupied, so you had your choice of yelling, "Anybody in there?" or pulling back one side of the blanket and taking a peek. The Toggery started out as a men's store, but recently Gordon's father had put in a line of bathing suits for women, so it was more important than ever to know who was behind the curtain. Most men

customers had given up yelling, "Anybody in there?" in favor of pulling back the blanket a little and taking a peek.

When I stepped out of the dressing room in my plus fours, feeling every inch a golfer, or at least every inch from my waist to below my knees, I was greeted by various reactions.

"Are they supposed to hang down so far?" asked my mother, a woman of limited experience who had never been on a golf course and had never seen anyone wearing plus fours.

"They're a perfect fit," said Gordon's father, "though we

may have to take them in a little at the waist." This latter remark was hardly necessary, because I was clutching my plus fours with both hands, and they would have dropped to my feet if I had let go.

"How much do they cost?" was, characteristically, my father's first thought.

As for me, when I saw myself in The Toggery's three-way mirror in those green-and-white plus fours, I was too overcome for words. My shoulders were as narrow as a fence slat, but, thanks to the generously billowing plus fours, looking for all the world as if I had stepped into two colorful gunny sacks, my thin legs and bony knees were cleverly hidden. For all anyone knew, they were as manly and well-proportioned as those of Rudolph Valentino or Douglas Fairbanks. Golf, obviously, was the game for me.

"Why do they call them plus fours?" my mother asked, breaking into my reverie just as I won the British Open and was accepting the cup personally presented by King George V.

"That's a good question," said Gordon's father, who, as usual, had some sort of seemingly plausible, and in this instance almost correct, answer on the tip of his tongue. "They're called plus fours because they hang four inches below the knee." Then he added, noticing that the green-and-white pair he was trying to get rid of hung eight inches below my knees, "At *least* four inches, I mean."

"I don't see why you can't play golf in a regular pair of pants," my father said grumpily. His question about how much the plus fours cost had never been answered, but he had groped around until he found the price tag. He wasn't going to ask again, and let Gordon's father think he was concerned about money, but there was no disguising the look of pain that came over his face.

"The trouble with trousers" (Gordon's father never said pants) "is that they restrict the knee action when you pivot. Plus fours were scientifically designed to give the golfer maximum freedom."

"Maximum freedom, hell," my father said, fighting hard to keep Gordon's father from making a sale. "Maximum freedom is something you'd get only if you played with no clothes on."

"Watch your tongue," my mother said, simultaneously elbowing my father in the side, at a point made tender by years of similar warnings. For once, Gordon's father had no retort, and we were all bemused for a moment, each in his own way picturing a nude golfer on the first tee, digging his toes into the grass, pivoting nicely, and then belting the ball and following through, all with maximum freedom.

"Everyone is wearing plus fours at the Club this season," said Gordon's father, the first to cast the unclad golfer out of his mind and get back to business. The thought of what nude golfing would do to business at The Toggery had shaken him briefly, but now he was determined to press on toward a sale. "Shall I take these up at the waist a little? I can have them ready for you by Saturday." He was already making chalk marks at the belt line, using his technique of keeping one step ahead of the customer until he had pulled him along to the point from which he could not retreat without embarrassment.

"Haven't you something in blue or brown?" my mother asked. "These seem a little bright."

"Of course I have other colors and patterns," Gordon's father said, "but green and white in plaid and large checks is the very latest. Chick Evans wore a pair very much like

16

these in the Western Open last week. You must have seen his picture in the rotogravure section."

Except for the nervous tic that started under my father's right eye when he heard the words "large checks," there was no further obstacle to the sale. Gordon's father had carried the day, and we could turn to the rest of my wardrobe. For the next three years, I was easily identified on the golf course by my green-and-white plus fours, though a little hard to find in the rough, where I blended with the foliage.

The remainder of my first golf outfit was purchased more quickly. My mother seemed unable to think up any further questions, and the fight had completely gone out of my father, who sat there with an opened checkbook, idly looking back through the stubs, each of them recalling some earlier defeat.

My first golf sweater, a slipover which I never remembered to slip on until I had carefully combed my hair, was brown, with large yellow diamond-shaped patches that formed what someone surely had considered an interesting design. In an indirect way, this sweater helped my golf, for the yellow patches, gazed at for a minute or so, had a dizzying effect on the observer, and usually added from five to ten strokes to my opponent's score. My socks were dark green, with inch-wide horizontal stripes that had the effect of making my lower legs seem to be chopped into segments which did not quite meet. They were eerie looking, all right, and caused bystanders to wonder how I managed to walk, much less play golf.

The shoes we chose were the black-and-white saddle type. Not until later was I to discover that taking care of such shoes is a full-time job. I used to polish the black part first, leaving a rim of black on the white part. Then I would polish the white part, leaving a rim of white on the black. Then I would remove the white from the black, which left a few streaks of black on the white, and then remove the black from the white, which left a few streaks of white on the black. This sometimes went on for half an hour, since I am a bit of a perfectionist. They were saddle shoes, all right, and I was saddled with them.

Spiked shoes were little worn in those days, but my red rubber soles gripped the ground very nicely with their deep tread, resembling that on a truck tire. I left a peculiar design wherever I walked, a series of concentric circles with an X in the very center. People could easily tell when I had passed by, and which way I was heading, merely by noting my spoor crossing a dusty road or an unswept sidewalk. It was a good thing I committed no crimes worse than crossing my mother's newly waxed floors, because even the stupidest policeman could have tracked me down.

As we left The Toggery with my golf clothes, all but the plus fours, which I was to pick up on Saturday, Gordon came in.

"All tricked out?" he asked.

"Yes," I said, wondering a little about who had tricked whom. I didn't hear the conversation between Gordon and his father after we had departed with our purchases. But I can imagine how it went.

"Did you do all right with those easy marks, the Armours?" Gordon must have asked.

"Well enough," his father probably said. "Remember those ghastly green-and-white plus fours I've had in stock two years and couldn't even give to the Salvation Army? So help me, they bought them for that puny kid of theirs and paid the full price. Two sizes too large, too. And they took those black-and-white saddle shoes."

"You don't mean the broken pair?"

"Yep, the ones with the 8½A right and the 9B left. I think he's too dumb ever to notice. Or maybe the drag to the left will make him walk around in circles. Come on, I think I'll close up early and go home and celebrate."

Chapter
Three

W hen I began to play golf, in the Old Days, I had
seven fewer than the maximum number of clubs allowable,
and so was never in danger of being disqualified in a tournament. Moreover, instead of merely being numbered, each
of my clubs had a name and, therefore, a personality. They
were a driver, a brassie, a spoon, a midiron, a mashie, a niblick, and a putter. All of them had wooden shafts. Steel had
been invented some years before, but it was still being used
for such nonessential items as skyscrapers, bridges, and auto-
mobiles. In a peculiar way, those wooden shafts affected my
golf game and, I suppose, my life, since my golf game and
my life were for many years inextricably bound to one another.

The first summer after I started to play golf, we took our
two weeks' vacation in the same leisurely way we had taken
it every summer for as long as I could remember. We picked
out a nice spot across a couple of mountain ranges and several
states that it would take us about six days of hard driving to
get to. Six more days of hard driving to get back left us two

days at our vacation spot, one of which was used for unpacking and the other for packing.

This summer I wanted to take my golf clubs along. Even if our schedule allowed no time for playing, I could get in a few practice swings when we stopped for gas.

"Of course not," my father said when I asked whether I could stow my golf clubs with the camping equipment. "If I had any extra space, I'd fill it up with a few more five-gallon cans of gasoline. It goes against the grain to pay forty-five cents a gallon in some of those out-of-the-way places in the mountains." Something was always going "against the grain" with my father, whose grain seemed to run in the opposite direction from most things and people with whom it came in contact.

"But I'll hold them in my lap," I pleaded. They were such lovely clubs, and I had had them only a few weeks.

"No," my father said, and I could tell he meant it.

So my golf clubs and I were separated during our two weeks' vacation. I left them in the safest place I could think of— in the basement leaning against an iron pipe in back of the water heater. If my parents had given me the choice, I would have stayed home that summer, and gone out every day to the Mountain Meadows Country Club and worked on some of the weaknesses in my golf game, which were mostly in my drives, long irons, short irons, approaches, and putts. But I was compelled to go on the vacation trip, and for fourteen days could do nothing but play imaginary rounds of golf, which soon became a monotonous string of birdies and eagles.

The vacation went about as usual, which meant that everything was bad: weather, roads, food, and tempers. Eventually, late Sunday night and without a spare because of a blowout only fifty miles from home, after all the filling stations were closed, we drove back into our driveway.

"It's good to be home, isn't it?" my father said, suddenly realizing, as he did at this point every year, how much better a vacation he would have had just lounging around in the back yard for two weeks, and how much he would have saved.

"I'll help unpack in a minute," I said, and hurried into the house and down to the basement to get my golf clubs. I wanted to take a few practice swings on the front lawn. The clubs were right where I had left them, leaning against the

pipe in back of the water heater, but they were dripping wet and the bag was soggy. I had left them under a joint in the hot water pipe that had been leaking directly into the bag for two weeks.

"Where's that boy?" I heard my father grumbling as I came

up from the basement. "I can't get all this stuff out of the car by myself." With that, he walked toward the house, carrying two left-over rolls of toilet paper in one hand and some road maps in the other. "Great guns!" I heard him exclaim to my mother as he stumbled over something by the front door. "Didn't you telephone them not to deliver the paper while we were away?"

It was after midnight when my mother and I finished unloading the car and my father caught up on the local news by reading the last of the fourteen newspapers, from time to time yelling to us about someone who had died. Only then could I get out onto the lawn and try some practice swings.

I expected to be a little rusty, after a two weeks' layoff, but I seemed to have lost my touch completely. As I swung one club after another, out there on the lawn in the dark, I could tell by the feel that I wasn't taking any turf. Could I have grown an inch or two on vacation, a sudden spurt that would make me almost as tall as Gordon?

"Get to bed," came my father's voice. "You're keeping me awake."

In the morning, when I pulled my mashie from the bag resting on the floor by my bed, like a slender brown dog sleeping by his master's bedside, I discovered that it was not I who had changed in two weeks, it was my clubs. The wooden shaft of each—not only my mashie but my driver, brassie, spoon, midiron, niblick, and putter—was curved like a sickle or a scimitar. All that leaning against the hot water pipe, dampened by the steady drip and kept warm by the heater, had warped every shaft into a half circle.

In the days that followed, I tried every possible way to straighten out those shafts. The first, clamping the clubhead of my midiron in a vise and steadily pulling down on the shaft, was the method I discarded most quickly, in fact as soon as the shaft snapped in two. Fortunately, I rarely used a midiron, and now I resolved to get more distance with my mashie or take a shorter swing with my spoon.

Other techniques, such as heating the club shafts in the kitchen oven, which had no ill effects other than to remove the varnish, and putting my clubs between my bed springs and mattress, a means I had long used for pressing my pants, were of small help. But gradually, one way and another, I managed to straighten out the shafts until they curved in only a shallow crescent, and people stopped staring at me, open-mouthed, when I drove off the first tee with what looked like a boomerang.

Fortunately, the clubs had all leaned in the same way against the water pipe, and the curves were fairly uniform. In a few weeks I learned to compensate for the curve in the shaft by bending somewhat lower and taking a shorter back-swing. My curved-shaft putter was actually an improvement, and it got so that perfect strangers would come up to me on the course and ask where they could buy one. Except for the putter, though, my clubs were good only for me. No one else had worked out the special swing, or developed the precise curvature of the spine, which made it possible to hit the ball instead of fanning above it or striking the ground two inches behind when over-compensating.

Of course I might have told my father what had happened to my clubs, the ones originally his, and asked him to buy me a new set. But I knew better. It was easier just to adapt myself to the clubs for a couple of years, until I was in college, when I could buy a new set of clubs with money I said was needed for books and lab fees.

When I eventually got new clubs, I had to readjust my

swing, and that bend in my spine never did go away, which explains my odd stoop, thought by most people a deformity I was born with. In with my new set of matched clubs I kept two unmatched ones. Indeed, they were not only unmatched but matchless. I refer to my curved-shaft putter and my equally curved-shaft mashie, a mighty fine club for playing an otherwise unplayable lie up against a tree. With this remarkable club I could stand behind a tree trunk and hit a ball nestled in front of it. Amazing as it looked, this was a fairly routine shot for me, since I was often in this situation. What I found more difficult, largely from lack of practice, was hitting a ball in the middle of the fairway.

Chapter
Four

At first I picked up what I could about golf by observing the better players at the Club, and imitating their swing. The only trouble was that even the best players at Mountain Meadows were none too good, and they had widely differing styles. For a while I slavishly imitated Ralph Yarborough, who had an unusually flat swing and closed his left eye. Ralph could get around in 86, when his putts were dropping, and this seemed little short of miraculous to me, my lowest score being 102, if I forgot a few strokes in the deep rough, where I was well out of sight.

Using the same flat swing as Ralph, and shutting my left eye tight, I confidently expected to break 90 any day, but I didn't. In fact I soared to around 120, even though I gave myself all the breaks, including conceding myself any putt under three feet.

"I can't understand it," I told Gordon one day. "I swing just like Ralph Yarborough and yet look at the difference in our scores."

"Ralph's swing is too flat," Gordon said, "but he has it grooved. Besides, he's stocky and you're skinny, and what's a good swing for him isn't necessarily a good swing for you."

"I've studied his swing for weeks," I said, "and practiced in front of a mirror. One little trick I've picked up from Ralph is closing my left eye, and you can't tell me the way we're built would make any difference about that." I had him here, and was a little caustic. It wasn't often I got the better of Gordon. "Did you say you close your left eye? Are you crazy?" Gordon asked incredulously.

"Well, yes," I said, meaning to answer his first question.

"Don't you know why Ralph closes his eye?"

"I suppose it's a way he has of helping his concentration," I said. "It seems to work."

"You poor fool," Gordon said. "Ralph's had trouble with his eyes all his life. They don't coordinate. When he looks down he sees double, unless he closes one eye. If Ralph could keep both eyes open when he swings, he'd be a par golfer."

"Oh," I said, "I see." And I stopped imitating Ralph Yarborough and began swinging at the ball with both eyes open again, and one day broke a hundred—made a 99, to be exact.

But I couldn't help watching the better players and picking up some mannerisms that I built into my swing. From Tom Garthside, for instance, I got the habit of coming to a dead stop for a second at the top of my backswing. In fact I improved on Tom, and held my club poised up there for a full two seconds before starting down. It was great form for a golfer who wanted his picture taken at the top of his backswing, but it took me three months to get over it and added about ten strokes to my score.

From Jack Larson I got a kind of preliminary waggle, more appropriate to a hula dancer than to a golfer, that I have never shaken—or perhaps I should say have never stopped shaking. It did my game neither harm nor good, though I think it helped steady me down. For a while my score, which had erratically fluctuated between 100 and 115, stayed pretty regularly at the latter figure.

From Ed Hughes I learned a putting stance that, likewise, did me no harm, partly because I gave it up after a bad fall. You see, Ed's putting stance involved standing well ahead of the ball and leaning toward the hole as far as possible. On a short putt, this meant looking directly into the hole and raking the ball in, like a croupier at a gambling table. Unhappily, it worked for no one but Ed, who had a peculiar center of gravity. As near as I could tell, he was kept from falling on his face because his left shoulder was counterbalanced by the large flask of whiskey he always carried in his right hip pocket.

Frankly, my game wasn't improving at all. The only reason I broke a hundred, just after I stopped closing my left eye, was that the fairways were baked, during a summer dry spell, and a topped drive would roll a good 200 yards, or even 250. Since a topped drive was my specialty, I was really getting distance that day. But the rains had come again, and it looked as if it would be a year, barring unseasonable weather, before I could count on another drought to lengthen my drives.

So I decided to take a lesson from the Club pro, Earl Foresman. Earl was a heavy-set, red-faced man with, as the saying goes, hands like hams. When I sought him out for a lesson, Earl was in the caddie house, figuring out the handicaps of club members, based on scores they had turned in. Mine was 36. Not that I could play to it, but this is as high as they went.

"I'd like a lesson, Earl," I said. "There are a few things I want to straighten out." One thing I wanted to straighten out was my drives, which were slicing so badly that they curved back almost to my feet, and I yelled "Fore!" at myself.

"If you want an hour, you'll have to wait until tomorrow, but I guess I can give you a half hour right now and get it over with," Earl said. There was a note of hostility in his voice. He had seen me hacking around the course with my curved clubs, and stayed away as far as possible. This was not only for safety's sake but because he had a sort of reverence for golf, and what I was doing was sacrilege. However, he had to eat.

"A half hour will be fine," I said, because I couldn't afford any more than that, anyhow. I wanted to save a little money for a box of those wooden tees that had just come on the market. I had picked up a few, and thought them a great improvement over the daub of damp sand generally in use to set up the ball for a drive. Besides, I found it hard to carry damp sand around in my pocket for teeing up the ball in the fairway when I needed to get distance with a brassie or spoon.

First, though, I had to pay. Earl liked to get his money in advance, because the list of "Members in Arrears" was a long one. As soon as financial arrangements were completed, we were off for the practice fairway, Earl lugging a canvas bag of balls and looking none too enthusiastic.

"All right, let's see you swing," he said when we were a safe distance from players on the course. From his tone I could tell he was expecting the worst.

I topped a few balls, some of them getting a pretty good dribble down the fairway.

"You're lifting your head," he observed, though I was absolutely certain I was not. However, I wasn't going to waste any of my half hour arguing.

"I'll watch it," I said, just to humor him.

"That would be hard to do," he said a trifle unpleasantly, "unless you're a Siamese twin. I've a better idea." Thereupon he took off his cap, which had a long bill on it, and handed it to me.

"I prefer to play bareheaded," I said. "I like the sun."

"Put this on," he said, and it sounded like an order.

So I put on his cap, though it was a quarter size too large and smelled of sweat.

"Now try a few shots with your mashie," he said, all business. "And don't worry about your head. I'll take care of it."

Just before I started my backswing, he reached up and grabbed the bill of the cap, which he held with a firm grip until I had hit the ball and finished my follow-through. When he let go, and I could look up, I saw that the ball had gone high and true, with a carry of 130 yards down the fairway. Usually I didn't get that far in the air with a driver, while my regular mashie shot was a shanked topper that skittered along the ground about 75 yards off to the right.

"Nothing wrong with that shot," Earl said. "Now let's try a brassie." I reached for some of the damp sand in my pocket, but Earl dropped a ball onto a level patch of grass and stepped forward to grab my cap. "If you keep your head down," he said, you can get loft with a wood from a decent lie on the fairway. "I've heard," he added, looking at me accusingly, "that some dubs around here are playing winter rules in July."

I shook my head sadly, agreeing with him that it was stupid, as well as against the rules, for anyone to tee up a ball in the fairway in midsummer. The damp sand hung heavily in my pocket as I picked up my brassie and took my stance, my feet turned inward at a forty-five-degree angle.

"What's the matter with your feet?" Earl asked. "I didn't know you were pigeon-toed."

"I stand this way for wood shots," I said. "It keeps me from over-swinging."

"Well, that's one I've never heard of," Earl said. "Another way to avoid over-swinging," he said, and I think there was a trace of sarcasm in his voice, "is to keep your hands in your pockets. Come on and hit the ball. You've got only ten minutes left out of your half hour." That was Earl for you. While I had been keeping my eye on the ball, he had been keeping his eye on his watch.

31

Once again, while I swung, Earl kept a tight grasp on the bill of my cap. My swing was a little cramped, with my pigeon-toed stance, and I lunged at the ball the way I always did when I was trying to get distance. But when Earl let go and I could look up, I saw my ball arching beautifully through the air, coming down a good 175 yards away, and rolling another 15 or 20. It was an awe-inspiring sight. For the first time since I took up the game, I had lofted a ball with a brassie from an ordinary lie on the fairway.

That one lesson did wonders for my golf. Now I could play a pretty good game, as long as I wore a cap with a long bill which someone held tightly while I swung. There were only two things that troubled me. One was that when I made a shot, under these circumstances, that was worth watching, I couldn't watch it. The other was that many selfish persons I played with were reluctant to perform this small but essential cap-holding service for me.

"You mean I have to walk all the way from my ball over to where you are, and hold onto your cap, every time you swing?" This was the question I was invariably asked by those who had not played with me before, when I made my modest request at the start of a round. In a foursome it wasn't so bad, one player usually being over in my part of the fairway. But in a twosome the person playing with me, unless he was also a slicer, had a little extra walking to do.

"You play golf for exercise, don't you?" I would ask shrewdly. "Well, this way you get twice as much." But many were unconvinced, or lazy. Some, I am sure, were willing enough to help me out, but cowardly. They didn't think it possible to stand close enough to a player to hold the bill of his cap, while he assumed a pigeon-toed stance and took a lunging full swing with a crescent-shaped driver—not without getting maimed.

Eventually I gave up having anyone hold the bill of my cap so I would keep my head down. It was too hard to get up a game, except with some new member of the Club, who was usually unavailable after our first round together. I tried drilling a hole through the bill of my cap and running a piece of heavy cord from my cap to my right foot, but the cord got in the way of my swing. The first time I went through with it, I wound up in a pathetic tangle on the first tee, lying on my face until a sympathetic onlooker cut me loose with his pocket knife.

There was only one other way, and I gave it a good try. I held the bill of my cap with my left hand while I swung at the ball with my right. Though this was not wholly successful, it gave me some idea of what it must be like to be a one-

armed golfer. I also learned how quick some people are to think other people peculiar.

I went back to playing golf bareheaded and swinging a club with two hands after Gordon told me about the petition. What Gordon said was that there was a petition going around the Club, requesting the Membership Committee to withdraw my membership because of "personal mannerisms which are distracting to other players and may, indeed, be indicative of a mental breakdown."

"You're making it up," I told Gordon. "Who in the world would ever get up a petition like that?"

"I don't know," Gordon said, "but it's the truth. I saw the petition yesterday, and it had twelve names on it already."

Gordon was right, because I got a look at the petition myself, when somebody left it for a few minutes on a bench in the locker room. When I saw it, there were twenty-three signatures.

And the first of them was Gordon's.

Chapter
Five

Though my father never played golf again, after that disastrous round with Gordon's father, he maintained a lively interest in the Mountain Meadows Country Club. It had cost him $300 to join, and this entitled him to a certain percent, or fraction of a percent, of the profits. It also gave him the privilege of sharing in any losses that might be incurred. He was, in short, a stockholder, and when it came to holding stock, my father clutched it with both hands.

For some reason, my father was not made a member of the House Committee, but committee membership was to him only a technicality. As a paid-up member, he had a perfect right to examine the architect's drawings of the clubhouse, before it was built, and to inspect the work of carpenters, painters, plumbers, and electricians while it was being constructed. Once the Club was in operation, he took it upon himself to oversee the making of soup and sandwiches in the Snack Bar.

"This needs a little more onion salt," he would say, as he dipped a ladle into the kettle of soup and tasted tentatively. The cook would stand back respectfully while my father puckered his lips and looked out into the distance as if trying

to recall the words of that great French gastronome, Brillat-Savarin. My mother insisted that my father had the taste of a peasant, for he enjoyed none of the more exotic recipes she attempted, and he resisted any variation from eggs and bacon for breakfast and pot roast and potatoes for dinner, day in and day out. But in the kitchen of the Mountain Meadows Country Club, he was an epicure with highly developed taste buds. After all, if anything went wrong at home, the worst that could happen was an upset stomach. But if the food wasn't just right at Mountain Meadows there would be a falling off of trade, and the Club was barely breaking even as it was.

In the pro shop, where he pinched balls (that is, squeezed them—he didn't steal them) and bent clubs ("Just testing," he'd murmur), what really caught my father's eye was the notices of club tournaments. More specifically, he was fascinated by the prizes: cups, plaques, statuettes, and occasionally something really useful, like twenty-five dollars in cash.

"Why don't you ever win a prize?" he asked me one day when I came into the Snack Bar for a lemonade, after shooting a creditable 52 on the front nine but a not-so-good 57 on the back nine, where I had become a little careless and counted up all my strokes on No. 16.

"I don't play quite well enough to win the low gross," I said, "and my handicap of 36 isn't enough to put me in the running for the low net." My father knew nothing about golf, but he understood gross and net from owning a drug store. Gross, to him, was of secondary importance. Net was what counted, since it was what he had left over after paying costs and overhead.

"Then it looks to me as if they should give you a bigger handicap," my father said. "Could you win if you had a 40 or 50?"

"Yes, I suppose I could," I said, "but 36 is as high as they go. It's the limit."

"It's the limit that you never win a tournament," my father said, "and bring home one of those prizes."

"Well, I'd like to have a cup to put in my room," I said.

"How about twenty-five dollars?" my father said. "You could put that in the bank."

"I'd rather have a cup," I said.

"Just try to sell one of those cups for twenty-five dollars," my father said. "I'll bet you couldn't get fifteen. Besides, you would always be having to clean off the tarnish. Better take the cash." (My father and grandfather were born in Ohio, but all of the earlier generations of Armours were born in Scotland.)

My father was deep in thought for a minute, not even noticing when the counter boy, a boy who wasn't much of a counter, put three olives instead of two on a plate with a cheese sandwich. Finally he spoke up. "They're going to give you a higher handicap, a 45 at least," he said.

"What makes you think so?" I asked.

"I'm going to tell them to, that's what," my father said, pressing his lips into a hard, fine line, as he did when he was determined about something. "I'm a stockholder here, and some of my money goes into those prizes. We should get our fair share back."

Despite his best efforts, which involved appearing before special meetings of the Greens Committee and the Tournaments Committee and the Subcommittee on Handicaps, my father was unable to get me a handicap above 36. He even threatened to sell his membership to some undesirable character who would embarrass the Club and cause trouble.

"Go ahead," said George Abernethy, Chairman of the Greens Committee, a man utterly devoid of tact. "Maybe it would be an improvement."

At that, my father stalked out of the committee meeting without a word, showing no emotion whatsoever except for his livid face, his rapid breathing, and his tightly clenched fists. He would have sold his membership in Mountain Meadows before nightfall to anyone, though preferably a paroled rapist, but the going price for a membership was temporarily down from the all-time high of $300 that my father had paid. He was offered $225, but, after thinking it over, decided he would rather stay in the same club with "that son-of-a-you-know-what, George Abernethy," than take a loss. He would make a tournament winner out of me yet, even with a measly 36 handicap, and show up that whole crowd of nitwits and poor sports.

To prepare me for tournament golf, my father said I could have all the lessons I wanted from Earl Foresman, though he charged twice what he was worth. But Earl, after a few lessons into which he never put much enthusiasm, gave up.

"I can't do anything more for you," he said. Since he had never done anything for me before, except to show me how to keep my head down if I could find someone who would hold the bill of my cap, I thought he was overstating his contribution to my game. I still had a ninety-degree slice, though I had tried dropping my right hand under the shaft, hitting from the inside out, using a square (as well as oval, or egg-shaped) stance, and holding the club loosely with my fingertips, this last resulting in my letting go of the club and throwing it through the window of the Snack Bar, which should never have been built so close to the first tee.

Unfortunately for me, Mountain Meadows was designed to persecute the golfer who sliced. There was a large untrapped area of the course, from the center of each fairway to the extreme left, which I, as an inveterate slicer, had never trod, in fact had never seen except from a distance. All the hazards were along the right side of the fairway—rough, traps, gullies, and, when there were tournaments, spectators. Had there been a river or lake in the vicinity, the course would have been laid out alongside it in such a manner as to provide a water hazard to the right of every fairway.

Though Mountain Meadows had no water hazard, I had once played a course that did have, on one hole, and had bought a "floater" just in case. A floater, for those who didn't play golf back in the Old Days, was a ball that floated, and

could be played if the water was shallow enough and you didn't mind getting a little wet to save a stroke. A stroke was so important to me that I would not only have waded to my floater but would have swum, if necessary. How I would have managed my stance and taken a full swing, in water over my head, I fortunately never had the need to figure out. This one time I played a course with a water hazard I stayed dry by going around to the right. Afterward I kept the floater in my golf bag along with my other balls on the chance they might some day put in a water hazard at Mountain Meadows. Or I might have to play over a puddle and not be sure of having enough carry. The floater had no life in it for ordinary play, partly because of the stuff it was made of to give it buoyancy and partly because I had bought it second-hand, for a dime, and it was no telling how many years old.

At my father's urging, I entered every tournament at the Club. "You're bound to win sooner or later," he said, "just by the law of averages."

On the same basis, I should also eventually make a hole-in-one, though not until I could reach the green of one of the three-par holes from the tee, which I hadn't managed yet.

I tried all the tournaments, including match play, in which I once got into the second round, thanks to a bye in the first; a flag tournament, a little flag being placed where each player made his last shot after taking 72 (par at Mountain Meadows) plus his handicap; and a whoop-and-holler tournament, when the idea was to try to rattle your opponent by making as much noise as possible while he was concentrating on his shot. In the flag tournament, the 108 strokes I was allowed took me so deep into the rough alongside the eighteenth fairway that they still hadn't found my flag three days after the tournament. In the whoop-and-holler deal, I was acknowledged the best at whooping-and-hollering, but they gave the prizes for low scores.

The only tournament I came close to winning was a one-club tournament, in which you could play around with one club of your choice. Most chose a midiron or a mashie, but I shrewdly selected a putter. I got remarkably good distance off the tees, much farther than I usually did with my driver, and would probably have won low net if I had been better on the greens, where my putter felt awkward and out of place.

Finally my father gave up all hope of my bringing home a prize. About the same time it occurred to him that he wasn't getting his money's worth out of his $300 membership, because it was a Family Membership, and I was the only member of the family playing golf.

"It says here, 'any blood relative,' and that would include Lester, wouldn't it?" my father said one night, after studying the fine print in the membership contract. "He is a relative, and he has plenty of blood, along with the fat. Lester is going to have to take up golf, whether he likes it or not. And I'll bet you a dollar" (this was only a figure of speech) "he can win one of those tournaments."

Uncle Lester, my father's brother, was six feet tall and weighed 230 pounds when he was in trim or 240 and up most of the time. He had plenty of leisure, for golf or anything else, because he had never held a steady job, or even an unsteady one, but was supported by my grandmother. She called him her "baby," a term that some thought inappropriate for a thirty-year-old man who weighed himself on the scales at the feed store. My father's idea was that Uncle Lester's sheer weight, after he had a few basic lessons from Earl, would enable him to wallop his drives so far that he could afford to flub a few approaches and putts. The committee would start him off with a 36 handicap, and he would improve so fast that by the time they readjusted handicaps, the first of the next month, he would have carried off the prize for low net.

Uncle Lester was neither my father's favorite relative nor, usually, his idea of a good investment. But golf would get him off the streets for a while, and the cost of a couple of lessons would still be less than the twenty-five-dollar prize. He was, quite obviously, our white hope, at least as far as winning a golf tournament was concerned. "At last," my father muttered, "we'll get some good out of that overstuffed do-nothing."

Uncle Lester took an instant liking to golf, since it was completely unproductive and bore no slightest resemblance to a job. And Earl Foresman took an instant liking to Uncle Lester, because he could, indeed, clobber the ball, whenever he managed to hit it. Besides, he was full of dirty stories, some of which Earl had never heard, and he told them so vividly that Earl was spellbound and sometimes forgot to keep watch for any lady golfers who might be getting within golf shot or, more important, earshot. In fact he liked Uncle Lester so much that he gave him a couple of free lessons "on the Q.T.," which I gathered was somewhere in back of the clubhouse.

Except for the distance he could get off the tees, Uncle Lester's game wasn't so hot, but with that 36 handicap he had a chance. There was even a possibility that if he sprayed the course with enough wild shots he might knock out his chief competitors. Anyhow, we entered him in the first tournament to come along. Scorning my warped equipment, Uncle Lester borrowed a set of clubs with straight shafts for the occasion, but he emptied all the balls out of my bag and picked out half a dozen of the shiniest. To climax this family enterprise, my father made a side bet of five dollars with Gordon's father, at odds of twenty to one. He was so sure of making a hundred bucks, in addition to the prize money, that he had a bank deposit slip all made out.

"I'm banking on this one," he said, waving the deposit slip and laughing over his pun until he went into a coughing fit and my mother whacked him on the back and sent me hustling for a glass of water.

It was a medal play, eighteen-hole tournament, with a cup for low gross and twenty-five dollars for low net. There was a rumor that this would be the last tournament with a cash prize, because the winners might, if this became known outside the Club, lose their amateur status. As a matter of fact my father fully intended to spread the word, if Uncle Lester won, both to keep others from winning money in the future, if we couldn't, and to be able to say we had a golf professional in our family.

Most of the best players had already played their rounds and turned in their scores when we got Uncle Lester out to the course on Sunday afternoon. He was the only 36-handicap golfer entered, since I decided to concentrate on following our contender around, along with my father, carrying his clubs, giving him tips, and cheering him on.

"Looks like a lead-pipe cinch for low net," my father said, after running down the list of scores posted at the caddie house. "George Abernethy" (his lips curled when he spoke the name) "is low with 82-14-68. With his thirty-six handicap, Lester can beat him if he shoots a hundred three, and with the distance he gets, even if he goes out of bounds a few times, that should be duck soup."

So we started off, Uncle Lester putting all his weight into a drive off the first tee that went 280 yards and, luckily, stayed in the fairway by ricocheting from a fence post. He was so close to the green that his topped mashie shot rolled fifteen feet from the pin and he was down in two putts for a par four. Our man was a little erratic for the rest of the front nine, making sixes on the three-par holes, where he got no advantage

44

out of his prodigious drives. But he birdied one of the long five-pars, and even with a lost ball and two out-of-bounds finished the nine with a 46.

"George Abernethy is still in the lead with his net 68," my father reported, hurrying back to the tenth tee after checking on scores. "You can win the tournament with a 57 on the second nine. Nothing to it." The satisfaction of beating George Abernethy was beginning to assume more importance in my father's mind than winning the twenty-five-dollar prize or the bet with Gordon's father. He looked feverish and was, obviously, not himself.

On that second nine, an odd thing happened. Uncle Lester was swinging at the ball as hard as ever, but he wasn't getting the old distance, and distance was what he depended on. His drives, instead of sailing out there 270 or 280 yards, were taking a high, lazy flight and traveling not more than 150. From where they stopped, since he had no finesse with the middle irons, Uncle Lester was helpless. Moreover, he was beginning to lose confidence.

"I'm laying into them as hard as ever," he said, "but they don't go anywhere. Must be something wrong with my timing." Not that he had the slightest idea of what timing was, but he had heard Earl use the word, and it sounded technical, like something in the motor of a car. He took a seven on the tenth hole, even though I improved his lie a little when his third shot trickled into a sand trap, by pressing down the sand around the ball with my foot until it perched up almost as if on a tee. If I hadn't done it, my father would have, and not nearly as neatly or as inconspicuously.

"Maybe you're not cocking your wrists," I said, trying to be helpful.

"Hit harder, you big slob," said my father, who knew nothing about the finer points of the golf swing and, in this instance, was a little short on brotherly love.

You'll have to give Uncle Lester credit for trying. Every time he swung at the ball he gave it all he had, and he had a lot, grunting and sweating and wrapping the club almost around his neck. But apparently he had lost his strength. He was like Samson after Delilah worked him over with the scissors. It was pitiful to see this big man swinging so mightily and getting such meager results.

Frustrated by his inability to get distance, Uncle Lester forgot the first principles of golf that Earl Foresman had taught him, and began to lift his head, bend his left arm, let his right arm come out from his side, and rock back on his heels. Hole by hole he disintegrated, winding up with a colossal 12 on the eighteenth. Instead of making the necessary, and apparently easy, 57, which would have given him a total of 103 and a low net of 67, he took a 70 on that catastrophic second nine, for a total of 116 and a net of 80.

George Abernethy won the twenty-five-dollar prize with his net score of 68. My father paid his five-dollar bet to Gordon's father, tore up the deposit slip, and swore off betting for life. Uncle Lester returned to his accustomed forms of loafing.

And I discovered, when I got my balls back and studied the deep cuts Uncle Lester had made in the cover of one of them, why he couldn't get any distance on that second nine. He had played all nine holes with the same ball, which was unusual for him—and it was my lifeless ancient floater, cut almost to its cork center. I never told either him or my father, since there seemed to be nothing to gain and neither of them knew what a floater was. Anyhow, we were through playing at Mountain Meadows, because my father sold our Family Membership. The man who had offered $225 for it was no longer interested, and the best he could get was $200.

I wish I could say the members of the Club gave us a farewell party or made some little gesture. As a matter of fact there was a gesture, but it was none too friendly. My father and I had cleaned out our locker and stowed everything in the car and were driving off. As we drove around the circular driveway, my father looked over his shoulder to see the Club one last time.

"The tinhorn crook!" I heard him exclaim, his face going white, and I looked back to see what was upsetting him. George Abernethy was standing just outside the Snack Bar, thumbing his nose in our direction.

Holding the wheel with one hand, my father vigorously thumbed his nose at Mr. Abernethy with the other, making one extra turn around the circular driveway in this posture, as if saluting while passing in review.

47

Then we both turned our eyes front, as we left the Club forever. I heard what sounded like a ball or a club hitting the rear of the car, but it may have been a rock from the gravel driveway.

"Don't look back, son," my father cautioned me. "Don't give them the satisfaction." What scene he may have glimpsed in the rear-view mirror has always intrigued me, and I have a lively imagination. But I knew better than to ask. Henceforth words like "hell" and "damn" might be permitted in our household, with sufficient provocation, but not "Mountain Meadows Country Club."

Chapter
Six

About a year after we gave up our membership in the Mountain Meadows Country Club—a year spent largely on public links, to which I became ever more firmly linked—I went to college, though, as I look back on it, I learned more hanging around the caddie house. One thing that kept me from taking full advantage of higher education was my struggle to get lower scores.

When I was in the car, about to start the big adventure and leave home for college, six miles away, my mother and father checked to see that I had packed everything essential.

"Have you your tennis shoes?" my mother asked anxiously.

"No," I said, "but I won't need them. I'm going to play golf."

"How about a notebook?" my father asked. "You'll have to take notes in class."

"I'll use the backs of old score cards," I said. "That will save money, and they're a convenient size."

My father nodded approvingly. Now and then I did something he considered sensible, and on rare occasions something like this, involving economy, that he had not even thought of

himself. I might yet be trusted to carry on the Armour tradition and the family motto of "A penny saved is a penny earned," which Benjamin Franklin had cribbed from one of my ancestors.

And so at last, after making sure that the heads of my woods were carefully protected by their hand-knitted covers, I drove off, waving gaily and trying not to reveal the wave of homesickness that swept over me. In the rear-view mirror I could glimpse my dear old mother (she had turned forty that fall) dabbing at her eyes with her handkerchief. They could not expect to see me until the next weekend.

I had not driven more than a mile, however, when I remembered something essential I had left behind. My golf gloves! It threw me into a panic to think of how my hands would blister without them. The pain I could bear, but blisters always made me flinch as I tightened my fingers on the downswing, and I shuddered at the effect on my score. I turned the car around and raced back.

My mother and father were happy to have me home again so soon. But, after the golf gloves were found, there was the heartache of parting all over again.

"Son," my father said, pathetically trying to keep me in the bosom of the family a little longer, "won't you have a last cup of coffee with us?"

It was lucky he said coffee, because I might otherwise have forgotten the tees I left on a shelf in my closet. How could I be so careless! Without them, I would have to go back to using damp sand.

Eventually, after two or three more false starts, I was off for college, where it was my good fortune to room with a young man, Don Warfield, who played golf approximately as well as I, and was pretty discouraged about it. We discovered how evenly we played on the first day of college, when we cut our afternoon classes to get in eighteen holes on the college course, a nine-hole affair which, I quickly learned, was like an eighteen-hole course when you played it twice. Instead of grass greens, however, it had black greens made of sand mixed with oil. When you got ready to putt, you took from the hole a marker consisting of a metal rod and a crossbar covered with heavy cloth. This served as a kind of broom, which you pulled from the ball to the hole, smoothing a path in the sand. Or, as I discovered, you could use the handle to cut a groove from your ball to the cup. Then the only way you could miss was not to putt hard enough, or to putt too hard and jump out of the groove.

Don, as I have said, played golf no better than I, but in every other way I recognized him as my superior. In appearance a Greek god, he had what are known as chiseled features, except for a slightly scornful curl in the upper right-hand corner of his lips, where the chisel had apparently slipped. With his shapely legs, he looked far better than I in plus fours, and his socks stayed up. Even more enviable, he could remember whole chapters of a book, word for word, after one reading, and was so sure of getting all A's that in his freshman year he bought a watch chain to have ready for his Phi Beta Kappa key.

The college golf course was within walking distance of our boarding house, and greens fees were included in the tuition. As for balls, Don lost very few, whereas I spent Monday mornings on the course and thereby found enough to last me through the week. I had to miss my English Composition, Elementary Spanish, and American History classes, but there was no time like Monday morning for finding all the balls lost on Sunday.

"Let's have some golf," Don would suggest on a Thursday afternoon, when he had no classes and I had only Biology lab.

"O.K.," I would say, since I had no heart, much less stomach, for dissecting a frog. It was not cutting into the warty creature that bothered me so much as the smell of the pickling solution in which it had been shipped, we were told, all the way from Florida. (I never stopped to wonder what was the matter with local frogs, though our instructor might have thought we would be less emotional about slicing up strangers.) Whether the solution had done something to the frog or the frog had done something to the solution, I do not know, but the resulting odor was nothing in which Florida could take pride.

As time went by, Don did not have to say, "Let's play golf" or "How about a game?" All he had to do was jiggle his golf

bag, making the clubs rattle, and I would get the idea. Within thirty seconds we would be out of the house and on our way to the golf course. If firemen could answer an alarm as quickly, millions of dollars of damage would be saved annually.

One thing that contributed to my efficiency was that I was always ready, wearing my golf sweater and plus fours and rubber-soled golf shoes at all times. I was the only student who invariably wore knickers to class, but since I was seldom in class I didn't attract much attention. There were some uncomplimentary remarks, however, about my lugging my bag of clubs to Required Chapel, after I found I had to attend because I had used up all my cuts.

Don and I usually started with the intention of playing nine holes and ended up playing twenty-seven or thirty-six. I was always sure I would do better on the next nine.

"Just one more round," I begged, though it meant we would miss dinner.

"Well, all right," Don said. It was not that he lacked enthusiasm for golf, but excessive reading as a small child had weakened his eyes, and it was hard for him to see after dark, even when I stood there with a flashlight while he putted.

Some of our late sessions on the golf course caused Don to oversleep the next morning and miss his early classes. But his professors overlooked such absences, assuming he was doing independent study. Some of them, indeed, were flattered that he found time to attend their lectures.

"How did I do this morning?" I overheard Dr. Dillsworth ask Don in the hall, after his lecture on Economic Background of the French Revolution.

"Fairly well," Don said, "though I think you could have pointed up Louis XIV's lack of confidence in his Minister of Finance, Jacques Necker."

"Perhaps I did pass over that a little too rapidly," said Dr. Dillsworth. "I'm sorry."

Not having Don's remarkable memory, except for golf scores, I must confess that my own absences were not viewed so favorably by the faculty. Indeed, my remaining in college must be attributed largely to two persons to whom I shall be eternally grateful. The first, of course, was Don, who had time on his hands, after doing his own work and playing golf four or five afternoons a week, to audit all my courses and fill me in on them.

"You really shouldn't, you know," I said.

"You are doing me a favor," he insisted. "They won't let me take more than six courses, but with my six and auditing your five I can keep reasonably busy."

I protested, but his will was stronger than mine. Besides, I feared the consequences if I denied him the chance to keep himself occupied. What if I forbade him to help me with my courses, and he drifted about aimlessly, fell in with bad companions, and got into serious trouble—something worse, even, than the trap in back of No. 7.

In the interest of my education and his peace of mind, we made a mutually agreeable arrangement which endured for four happy years, until I graduated with a B.A. and an 18 handicap. Don was to permit me to write my own term papers, though he could have written them far better, and in return I was to allow him to lecture to me on philosophy, economics, English and American literature, religions of the world, biology, and art, and to brush me up on Spanish grammar and vocabulary, while we were playing golf.

When I told my father I would take notes on the backs of score cards, I didn't realize how accurately I had spoken.

"What will it be today?" Don asked me on a typical afternoon, as he stood on the first tee, preparing to drive.

"Well, I have a test tomorrow on the economic theories of John Stuart Mill," I replied.

"All right," Don said briskly, as he teed up his ball and started his backswing, "I'll give you a summary of Mill's *System of Logic* on the first nine and review the basic concepts" (he hesitated a moment to watch his ball in flight, since it had a hook that might get him into trouble) "of his utilitarianism. It will probably take me another eighteen holes to run through Mill's *Principles of Political Economy* for you, if I'm to do it justice." Then, with a sigh of relief, "Boy, another foot and I'd have gone out of bounds onto the third fairway. Guess I'm standing too far in back of the ball. Now John Stuart Mill, who was born in London in 1806, tried to help the English working people by promoting measures leading to. . . ."

The other person to whom I was deeply indebted was Dean

Nickerson. Because of my irregular class attendance and the disturbance I made at Chapel when I arrived late and clattered down to the front row (we were seated alphabetically, rather than in order of piety) with my golf clubs, I avoided him as much as possible. As I recall, we had had no personal contact since the end of my freshman year, when he rejected my petition to major in Golf. Physical Education was possible, but Golf, apparently, was too specialized. As the President of this liberal arts college said (each year) when addressing the opening convocation, "You are here to learn to live, not to learn to make a living." There seemed to be some fear that I would become a golf professional instead of something more cultural, such as a high school P.E. teacher. Of course if I had thought there was any chance of my becoming a golf pro, I would gladly have quit college at once. But a person who had played golf for three years and yet whose best score was a 92, made while playing alone, was not likely to qualify in the near future for the U.S. Open.

About noon one Monday, the beginning of my junior year, when I came into my room after scouring the course for golf balls, Don handed me an envelope. I did not at first notice the alarmed look on his face, being so eager to report an unusually successful morning.

"I found six balls," I exulted, "one of them a brand-new Kro-Flite that hadn't been hit more than a couple of times."

"You'd better open that envelope," he said, pretty tense. Obviously he knew the nature of the contents, because he had rather clumsily resealed the flap. For all Don's amazing knowledge, he never learned to pry open an envelope and seal it up again without detection. Espionage was almost his only weakness, aside from a tendency to hook.

The envelope contained a note from the Dean, requesting

me to come to his office as soon as possible. It was terse, un-revealing, and, it seemed to me, ominous.

"What have I done?" I asked.

No answer came from Don. He was busy with a pencil and a large sheet of paper, scribbling numbers and mathematical formulae. It seemed heartless of him, at such a time, to be working out a problem in Advanced Calculus, even if it was his favorite subject.

At that moment he looked up. "I've got it!" he exclaimed excitedly.

"You've got what?" I asked, not caring much, since he seemed so little interested in something of immediate concern to his roommate and golfing partner.

"I've figured out the odds on your being tossed out of college," he said. "They're 896,231 to one that you'll get the axe. Of course that's rounded out to the nearest whole number. This can be proved by multiplying—"

Leaving him happily figuring, I hurried off to the Dean's office. Using the Scout's pace (fifty running, fifty walking), I was there in no time, or, to be more precise, in eight minutes.

"The Dean is expecting you," his secretary said. "But he is on the phone just now."

While I waited, trying to appear interested in back issues of *The Journal of Higher Education, School and Society,* and *Educational Digest,* I ran through the possible causes for my summons. Had Russ Allen, who had extra cuts to spare, failed to move over one place and sit in my seat at Chapel last week, while I was up on the course practicing chip shots? Had someone recognized Don's prose style in that last paragraph of my paper on "The Symbolism of *Moby Dick,*" when I had got stuck for a good ending?

"He's off the phone now," the secretary said, and I had a

quick vision of the Dean having been sitting on the phone for the past fifteen minutes, for some reason known only to educators, and now having resumed his place in his chair. "You may go in."

After a few pleasantries, the Dean got down to business. "You play a good deal of golf, I hear," he said.

"Well, I play a little," I said. "I take it for P.E."

"I understand you play almost every day," the Dean said.

"Perhaps I *have* been playing too much," I said. "I promise to cut down on it."

"Oh, no, don't do that," the Dean said quickly. "It doesn't seem to be interfering with your studies. Your work is quite competent. In fact Professor McCush told me only yesterday that you had written an excellent paper on the symbolism of *Moby Dick,* with a remarkably discerning and well-expressed final paragraph."

"Thank you," I said, wondering when he would get around to those Chapel cuts.

"What I called you in for is a very personal matter," he said, "and I must ask you to keep it in strictest confidence."

"Certainly, sir," I said. Chapel cuts were a personal matter, all right—between a man, his God, and his Dean.

"Well, there is to be a faculty-trustee golf match a week from next Saturday, ten members of the faculty against ten trustees, the losing team to buy a dinner for the winners. It's very important that we show the trustees we're still—uh, well —alive. I seldom have time for golf, but they had trouble rounding up ten faculty members, and though I am officially classed with the administration, I *do* teach one course, you know, to keep my hand in."

"Yes, I know," I said. The course he taught was "Educational Testing," popularly known as "Education 156a,b," in which there was usually an enrollment of four or five students, all of them girls, and homely.

"Now about this faculty-trustee match," the Dean went on, "I hate to let the faculty down, and my putting is a little off. When I heard you played golf so much, I thought you—that is, if you can spare me a few minutes and it's not an imposition— might look at my putting form and give me some tips."

"I'd be glad to," I said.

Thereupon the Dean brought out a putter and a couple of balls from a closet, where they had been stashed behind his academic regalia, and we had a session right there in his office, the Dean putting into a circular design in the center

of his rug while I analyzed his weaknesses. He wasn't bad at all, in fact he was a whole lot better than I was, but I didn't let on and didn't do any putting myself. I coached him as if I were the other Armour—Tommy—and getting ten dollars a lesson. With increasing confidence in my instructional ability, I showed him how to hold the blade of the putter in front of the ball to get lined up, explained the importance of keeping his weight even on both feet and swinging with a pendulum motion, and cautioned him about keeping his head down and following through. But the Dean didn't really need any lessons. He was a natural, with an uncanny sense of distance and direction, two very useful elements in putting. All he needed, besides a little confidence, was to get the stiffness out of his back so he could bend over.

For the next week I went to the Dean's office every afternoon, after his secretary had left, and put him through his paces. The only thing he ever said about Chapel was that he had always been opposed to requiring it, and was recommending that it be made voluntary next year. My admiration for the Dean as an educator was exceeded only by my admiration for the way he could concentrate on a putt. Now and then the phone rang just as he was starting his backswing, and he stroked the ball without faltering, apparently oblivious of the jangling bell, even though it might have been a call from the Prexy, or from his wife.

During our daily half hour together, the Dean was a single-minded man, and that single mind of his was wholly on putting. He was beginning to wear down the nap of the rug, in a line from the outside edge to the center of the design that served as the hole.

One afternoon, with the faculty-trustee match only two days off, the Dean was holding his hat in one hand and his bag of clubs in the other when I arrived at his office.

"Let's go over to my house today," he said. "I've mowed and rolled the back lawn and sunk a tin can in a regulation-size hole. It's time to leave this rug and get the feel of the green. Besides, I want to watch you do a little putting, and study your stroke."

I had been afraid of this. It was one thing for me to tell him what to do and quite another for me to demonstrate. If he learned what a lousy putter I really was, I'd be ruined, and just when he had asked me to stop saying "Dean Nickerson" and to call him Ben. I thought of saying I was sick, but I looked far too healthy, tanned as I was from my almost daily golf, and had bounced into his office full of gusto for the lesson I was about to give.

There was no way out, except through his window and southward down College Avenue, at a run, until I crossed the border, where I might continue my education at the University of Mexico. Meekly, I walked with the Dean to his home, carrying his bag and pulling my cap down over my face so that I would not be recognized by my fraternity brothers, who would surely put a club-carrier for the Dean in an even lower category than an apple-polisher for a professor.

The Dean was no golf architect, but he had made a very respectable one-hole course, or one-green course, out of his back lawn. As soon as we arrived, he dumped some balls on the grass, assumed his putting stance, and while I delivered a stream of cautions, congratulations, and technical advice about overspin and relaxed grip and roll of the green, smoothly stroked ball after ball toward the hole. He seemed to have forgotten about wanting me to demonstrate.

"Here, you show me," he suddenly said, handing me his putter. "I want to watch someone who really knows how."

This was it, the Moment of Truth. As I took the club from him, I was grateful for my billowing plus fours, which did not betray the trembling of my thin legs far inside. Other than cracking my knuckles one time around, I managed to control my nervousness as I stood over the ball and lined up a thirty-foot putt. If my lips moved slightly, it was because I was uttering a silent prayer: "Dear God, if you help me get this putt within a foot of the hole I'll never cut Chapel again."

Still praying, I closed my eyes and struck the ball firmly. When I opened my eyes, I saw I had hit the ball far too hard and off at a right angle. Miraculously, though, it caromed off the Dean's golf bag, which also took some of the force out of it, and came to rest six inches from the hole.

"Bravo!" the Dean cried. "You figured it just right. What a beautiful way to take advantage of a rub of the green, and to get around a possible stymie."

"Well, Ben," I said, as soon as I realized the Dean was sincere and not being sarcastic, "a straight putt to the hole would have been too easy, from this distance. But I really should have sunk it. I had the line, but I didn't hit it quite firmly enough. Never up, never in, as I always say."

"Let me see you do it again," the Dean said, "so I can get the shot better in mind, though I doubt that I can ever manage it myself."

"I'd be glad to," I said. Then I added, considerately, "But I don't want to take up too much of your time with my own putting. It would be selfish of me. With the match only two days off, we need to give you every possible chance to practice."

Before the Dean could repeat his request, I returned the putter to him and drew his attention to the slight roll-off to the left of his lawn and the need to study the direction the grass bent. In a moment he was so completely engrossed, hitting ball after ball first with and then against the grain of the grass, that he did not ask me again for a demonstration. "Thank you, God," I whispered, rolling my eyes upward when the Dean had his back to me, lining up an eight-footer.

The faculty-trustee match came off as scheduled, and the faculty won. It was close, though, and it all depended on the Dean, who came through like a champion, one-putting the last four holes and winning 3 and 2.

"I have you to thank," the Dean told me the day after the match. "You certainly did wonders for my putting, and I shall never forget it."

With customary modesty, I protested briefly before taking all the credit. In my last two years of college I could do no wrong, as far as the Dean was concerned.

But for Dean Nickerson, I doubt that the college authorities would have permitted me to carry my mashie onto the platform during the graduation exercises. It was not that I wanted something to toy with, but I was building up strength in my wrists, to help my iron shots.

There may have been some in the audience who wondered what, if anything, I was wearing underneath my gown, with no trouser legs showing below. Knickers, of course.

Chapter
Seven

As the years went by, after college, everything seemed to progress naturally. I married, had children, and once in a while broke 90. The only thing that might be considered a trifle unnatural was my practicing indoors.

Putting on the carpet my wife didn't mind, except when we had guests and I kept asking them to lift their feet. It was

the chip shots into, or in the general direction of, the waste-basket that got on her nerves.

"I don't mind your hitting the ball," she said, "but *must* you hack a piece out of the carpet every time?"

"It's not a piece," I said, trying to teach her the rudiments, or at least the nomenclature, of golf, "it's a divot. And if I don't take a divot I won't get any loft or backspin." She was a fine woman, in many ways, but she had a strange sense of values.

My indoor long iron shots and drives, even though I limited myself to practice swings without a ball, annoyed her fully as much. I must admit I went a little too far (about six inches) when I knocked over the lamp she inherited from her grand-mother, the one (the lamp, not the grandmother) with the delicately carved porcelain base. Of course I apologized and promised to clean up the mess as soon as I finished a few pitch shots. It had been an understandable miscalculation. I had carefully gauged the space required for my follow-through, but had forgotten about my backswing.

"I'm sorry," I said, as I switched from my driver to a No. 9 iron, "but accidents will happen. It was really a good break, though, because it showed that I'm over-swinging, and I might not have known otherwise. I can hardly wait to get out onto the course and see what happens when I shorten my swing."

Another bit of good luck was when I misjudged my follow-through with a No. 2 iron and imbedded the club in the wall. The clubhead penetrated the plaster and lath and came out in the next room. If my wife's sister, who was visiting us at the time, had been sitting up straight instead of bending over to pick up a pair of scissors from the floor, I might have killed her. It was as close as I ever came.

"See," I said, as I walked into the other room and pulled

66

my club on through. "I've always maintained we got gypped by the builder. It's lucky I discovered how flimsy these walls are before the house falls down on us."

I did not always practice indoors—only in bad weather and in the middle of the night, when a sudden thought came to me about what I had been doing wrong, such as opening the club face too much or uncocking my wrists a trifle early. Most of my practicing was on our back lawn, until there was not enough grass left to get a decent lie, when I shifted to the front lawn. After the front lawn gave out, I was forced to use a rubber mat in our driveway and hit the ball against the side of our house, the side where we ultimately boarded up the windows. People who drove past thought we were away for the winter, unless they saw me out there practicing.

My interest in the sport at length began to be noticed around town, notably my habit of reading a book on golf while driving the car, which some thought peculiar and others dangerous. But I had discovered a way of propping up the book on the steering wheel, and the only time I did not use both hands for steering was when I turned the page. The biggest stir I made was the time I stopped at the traffic signal at Second and Garey, and became so absorbed in a new book by Ben Hogan that I didn't notice when the light changed from red to green. Motorists behind me honked their horns and, after a few seconds, leaned out and yelled insults. I read on, fascinated by Hogan's explanation of how to hit the ball on a downhill lie. So preoccupied was I that I failed to see the policeman walking toward me from the center of the intersection.

"What's going on here?" he asked as he walked up to my car. And then, "Oh, it's you, professor."

"Hello, Mike," I said. It was Mike Grady, who was not only

a fine figure of a policeman but a member of my regular Sunday foursome. "I'm reading what Ben Hogan says about hitting the ball from a downhill lie."

"What does he say?" Mike asked, leaning in through the car window.

"It's all in the stance," I said. "Let me show you." I got out of the car and stood on the white line in the center of the road, placing my feet as Hogan instructed and taking a swing with an imaginary club. Cars were lined up behind me for a block, but no one honked or yelled, now that a policeman had taken charge. Drivers watched curiously, and a little sympathetically. I suspect they thought I was being given a sobriety test.

"That looks good," Mike said, placing his feet on the white line in the same position, and taking a very creditable swing

with his nightstick. "Well, we'll give it a try on Sunday. See you at the first tee at eight-thirty."

"So long, Mike," I said, getting back into the car and propping up my book on the steering wheel, ready to start the chapter on "Using the Sand Wedge." I drove off, and Mike motioned to the long line of cars to get going. At least they thought he was motioning them on, as he stood there on the white line, but it looked to me, in the rear-view mirror, as if he was working on that stance and swing of Hogan's.

Though life was generally sunny, one cloud loomed on my horizon: I was being forced into a financial dilemma. On the one hand, I could no longer give my Monday mornings, as I had in college, to looking for lost balls; on the other, I could not afford the cost of new balls, my ninety-degree slice having persisted for all these years. But an even greater dilemma

faced me one morning when my wife suddenly burst into tears.

"What's the matter, dear?" I asked. "Are you thinking about the trouble I had on the twelfth hole yesterday? Maybe I shouldn't have told you about it."

"No," she said, "it's more serious than that. It's about our married life."

Our married life? What, I thought to myself, has she to complain about? Haven't I been a good provider, keeping our dues paid up at the country club? Haven't I offered to let her take as many golf lessons as she wished, and is it any fault of mine that she has never taken up the game? I've showered her with jewelry—a pin made of two gold tees, expensive pendant earrings (cute little gold golf balls), and a charm bracelet hung with a tiny gold medal for each time I broke 90, with the date on it. What more could she want of me?

"Just what is the trouble?" I asked.

Instead of answering, she cried harder than ever. Her tear-stained face suddenly filled me with sadness, and I understood why. It looked like a golf course about which I had once had a nightmare, one with streams that ran along the right edge of every fairway and in front of every green. I shuddered, and put the ball I had been bouncing, to test for resilience, back into my bag.

"This can't go on," she said at last. "You'll have to choose between golf and me. Either you break yourself of the golf habit and quit entirely or I'm leaving you." She had braced herself for a moment, but now she broke down completely, and those streams once again ran all over the course.

What a choice to have to make, between golf and my wife! If she had just given me some time to think, instead of springing it on me this way. Until now, my most difficult choice had been between a No. 7 and a No. 9 iron, or whether to go over or around a sand trap.

As the desperation of my plight swept over me, I instinctively grabbed up my golf bag and clutched it to my breast, desolated by the prospect of giving up almost all that was dear to me. The bag, as I hugged it tightly, felt hard and ribbed, and the clubs inside rattled against one another like metallic bones. My wife was sobbing gently, certain that I had given her up. On an impulse, I dropped the clubs and embraced her, holding her tightly to me. It was amazing how much better she felt—soft instead of hard, and no rattling! My choice was made.

"Dear," I said, "I'm giving up golf."

Great was the rejoicing in my family when my decision became known. As the news rapidly traveled through the neighborhood, the Sanfords, who lived next door, came onto our property for the first time in years, no longer fearful of being struck by a ball exploded out of my daughter's sand-

box. In an outwelling of friendship, the Murchisons, who lived on the other side, promised to take down their spite fence within twenty-four hours. One elderly lady whom I hardly knew, but whom my wife apparently saw at church, while I was out on the course, said something that touched me deeply.

"I have been praying for you," she said, and I could see she thought this was what had turned the trick.

But I had not counted on the damaging inroads the game had made. I did not know how far gone I was. In a matter of hours I became aware of the frightful struggle that lay ahead, as the torment of withdrawal began to hit me. Though my golf clubs and golf attire had been quietly removed and, I doubt not, ceremonially burned, my memories remained to haunt me—memories of the smell of freshly mowed fairways, the feel of turf underfoot, the sound of clubhead meeting ball, the sight of a white sphere arching through the air and dropping on the green, even though it might then roll across and into a trap.

As the first horrible days dragged by, I ran the gamut of nervous habits—fingernail biting, head scratching, knuckle cracking, teeth grinding, muttering to myself. But nothing gave me relief. With shame and humiliation I confess that more than once I backslid, sneaking out to the golf course, breaking into a locker, and furtively playing a round, driven by an irresistible compulsion. Afterward I suffered the pangs of remorse and disgust, as I paid for the cost of the locker door I had jimmied off.

"Why don't you join G.A.?" my wife asked hopefully.

So I tried Golfers Anonymous, where golfers confessed their addiction and helped one another to go straight (something I had tried for years to do, but there was always that

slice). Each of us in G.A. was given the telephone number of a "brother" who could be called any hour of the day or night, when the temptation became unbearable. My own brother was an excitable Italian, Joe F., a barber who had been forced to give up golf when he almost cut the nose off a customer he was shaving. Joe had momentarily fallen into a reverie in which he imagined himself playing out of the deep rough, and it is a wonder the violent upward swing of the straight-edge, from just under the lathered gentleman's lower lip, required only a few stitches instead of plastic surgery.

I telephoned Joe only once, a little after midnight, when I felt I could not hold out until morning. I had watched a golf match on TV that afternoon, and tension had been building minute by minute. At dinner I had used two hands, and an overlapping grip, to hold my spoon, and had chipped a couple of peas from my plate into my coffee cup. That night, as I lay in bed, a myriad of tiny white golf balls danced before my eyes.

Feverishly, I dialed my brother's number. "Joe," I cried into the phone, "come at once. I need you!"

My G.A. brother was at my bedside within ten minutes, wearing a raincoat over his pajamas. He had come halfway across town, and must have driven with reckless abandon, or with a police escort.

Joe got me through the night, taking my mind off golf by telling me stories of his family and boyhood in Sorrento, and singing songs like "O Sole Mio" and "Napoli." But what mostly distracted me from golf, and at the same time determined me not to call my brother again, even in the most desperate plight, was the straight-edge he held clenched in his right fist all the while, nervously stropping it against his left palm. Sometimes he stopped his story-telling or his singing for a minute and sat in silence, staring across the room. The light from my bedlamp reflected on the gleaming blade, and I cupped my hand protectively over my nose.

Eventually I did as most members of G.A. did. In my effort to forget golf, I drank so heavily that I was forced to drop out, instead of staying with the cure, and transfer to membership in AA.

So it went. Who suggested a psychiatrist, I cannot recall, but nothing else remained. Even I could see now—with my head always down, as if to keep my eyes on the ball, and with my hands gripping an imaginary club—that I was a sick man.

"Whom shall I go to?" I asked one morning while shaving. I had assumed an open stance and was seeing how few strokes I could take to get around from one sideburn to the other.

"They tell me Dr. G. Lindley Smythe, in the city, is the best anywhere," my wife said. "And you are going to need the best."

I was in no condition to argue. An appointment was made, and within a fortnight (two weeks) I was being ushered into Dr. Smythe's office. As I entered, the doctor, who had been reading the file on me, rose from his desk to shake my hand and put me at ease. He was a tall, bearded man, wearing thick glasses and immaculate in a well-pressed white jacket.

"You have a golf neurosis, I see," the doctor said.

"I'm afraid so, doctor," I said, "and I've tried every possible cure."

"Tut tut," the doctor said, "there is always a chance to be cured if you really want to be. Now come over here and lie down on this couch while I take a look at your psyche."

I started to disrobe but then realized that this was not necessary.

"Now close your eyes," the doctor said. "When was it you began to play golf?" he asked.

75

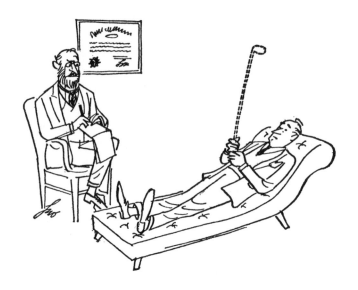

"About thirty years ago."

"Tell me how it began, everything you can remember." The doctor's voice was soothing, almost hypnotic, and vaguely familiar.

I went back to the beginning and told about that day on our front lawn and Gordon and the sprinkler holes and my father's unlucky game with Gordon's father and The Toggery and the green-and-white plus fours and my warped clubs and all the rest. I held back nothing, except some of my poorer scores.

"Have you ever had any suicidal impulses?" the doctor asked.

"Only after a bad round," I said.

"Have you ever wanted to murder anyone?"

"No, I don't think so."

"Are you sure? Try hard to remember."

"Well, maybe I have," I said.

"Who?" the doctor asked, or perhaps he said "Whom?"

This must have been a crucial and revealing question, because he suddenly seemed eager and expectant, and he was breathing a little harder.

"Gordon," I said. "Gordon Smith, the one who got me started on golf. Yes, I wanted to murder him and I still do, whenever I think about him."

At this point I became so overwrought that, though the doctor had not instructed me to open my eyes, I did so, and looked straight into the bearded face a few inches above mine and peering at me intently. I had a strange feeling. Perhaps I was losing my mind.

"Dr. G. Lindley Smythe," I muttered. And then, addressing myself to the psychiatrist and taking a long chance, "Doctor, is your first name Gordon?"

"Yes," he sighed quietly.

For the first time in months my hands relaxed their overlapping grip and took the position preparatory to strangulation of a victim.

"I am Gordon Smith," he said. "You would find out sooner or later." Then, seeing me rise from the couch and advance toward him with clutching hands, "Calm yourself. Give me a minute to explain."

Always a believer in fair play, I paused. Moreover, Gordon was larger than I, as he had always been, and the beard protected his neck.

"Look around you," he said, pointing with a sweeping gesture at his office. For the first time I noticed a bag of golf clubs leaning against his desk, golf balls scattered over the floor, and divot-size holes in the carpet. By now Gordon had a No. 9 iron in his hands, but not, apparently, to protect himself. He was chipping ball after ball at the wastebasket, with fierce intensity, saying not a word until one finally went in, whereupon he seemed to relax, as though a powerful spasm had passed.

"I, too, have a golf neurosis," he said, taking out his handkerchief and wiping beads of perspiration from his brow. "But unlike you, I am incurable, according to my psychiatrist. Kill me if you wish," he said, handing me a No. 2 iron, "but you will get sweeter revenge by letting me live. And remember," he said, "I can tell you how you can be cured, though I myself am beyond help."

For a moment I held the No. 2 iron like a rapier before me, as it flashed through my mind that in a duel to the death with Gordon I would have the advantage of three inches over the shorter shaft of his No. 9, more than compensating for his longer arms. Then a shudder went through me and I allowed the club to come to rest on the floor. The old hatred had gone, and now I felt only pity for Gordon, the incurable—doomed to live out his remaining years hitting golf balls against the walls of his padded cell.

"You say you know how I can be cured," I said.

He sighed with relief, and then, brightening, became crisply professional. "The cure for you is sublimation. Do you understand?"

"In a general way," I said. "Be more specific."

"What you must do," he said, "is to sublimate your craving for golf by turning your attention and energy to something else. How about carving ship models?"

"No," I said, "I usually cut myself carving a roast."

"Then why not play bridge?"

"My wife wouldn't stand for it. I always forget which trumps are out. In fact I usually forget what are trumps."

"Haven't you any other avocation?" he asked, beginning to lose hope.

"Well, I write a little light verse," I said.

"Good," he said.

"Not very good, I'm afraid," I said, "but the best I can do."

"That's it," he said. "If you can't play golf, write about it. Every time you have the urge to pick up a golf club, pick up your pen instead, and write a poem about golf."

"Thank you, Gordon," I said. "I feel like a new man already." I could hardly wait to get home and start writing, the first time I felt the impulse to swing a club.

"And take this along with you," Gordon said. He had been scribbling on a slip of paper, I presumed a prescription for a sedative, which he folded and handed to me.

Gordon's cure worked. I haven't touched a golf club in ten years.

But now my compulsion to write verses about golf is as strong as my old compulsion to play golf ever was. I carry a pencil and a writing pad at all times, for without them I would open a vein and write with my finger or a matchstick upon the bark of a tree. At the end of the day my pockets are stuffed with verses, which I dump out on the living room table when I get home. Since I write more light verse about golf than could possibly be published (there being a limited market), our attic and cellar are filled with boxes and bales of the stuff, and there is little room left for clothes in our closets. If all the verses I have written were laid end to end from the first tee to the eighteenth green, I could walk on a thick mat of paper, and my feet would never touch the grass. A few of these thousands of verses are included in the pages which follow—one way to clear a little space in the garage.

In short, thanks to the psychological technique of sublimation, I am completely free of the urge to golf but have become a light-verse-writing neurotic. And I am spending far more for paper than I ever did for golf balls.

Oh yes. The day after I was in Gordon's office I stopped in at a drug store and handed the druggist the slip Gordon had given me.

"I'd like this prescription filled," I said. The druggist took it from me and left me waiting. He was back in a few seconds.

"This is no prescription," he said irritably. "Are you trying to pull my leg?"

I took up the paper he had thrown down on the counter before me. Gordon, or G. Lindley Smythe, M.D., had written: "Professional services: $50."

I smiled wickedly. It was a bill I was happy to pay. Gordon's next ten rounds would be on me, and I hoped they helped hook him for good.

A round of golf
in verse

ABC OF GOLF

A is for *apron,* just short of the pin,
From which you can often take four to get in.

B is for *ball,* dimpled pellet of rubber,
That's smacked by the champion, hacked by the dubber.

C is for *caddy,* who trudges the course
With a burden of clubs that would weary a horse.

D is for *dub,* poor misguided beginner,
With visions of someday becoming a winner.

E is for *exercise,* needless to pay for,
Yet all that some golfers insist that they play for.

F is for *fairway,* inclined to be narrow
And bordered by bad lands that chill to the marrow.

G is for *green,* that's constructed to roll
In every direction away from the hole.

H is for *handicap,* sweeter than candy,
A cap that, when needed, comes in very handi.

I is for *ignorance,* excellent reason
For breaking a ground rule you've known of all season.

J is for *jitters,* a state you and I
Get in when it takes a two-footer to tie.

K is for *knees,* that unhappily tend
Each year to get harder and harder to bend.

L is for *locker,* which clothes that are kept in
Come out of as wrinkled as if they'd been slept in.

M is for *money,* expended with ease
On lessons and golf carts and golf balls and fees.

N is for *nineteenth,* the hole that's the best,
And the reason some golfers play all of the rest.

O is for *Open,* the tourney of stars,
Who shoot mostly eagles and birdies and pars.

P is for *par,* which is golfers' perfection,
Achieved by a union of length and direction.

Q is for *quiet,* desired when you putt up,
A time when the courteous clammily shut up.

R is for *rough,* a weird species of jungle,
Into which you go traipsing whenever you bungle.

S is for *score,* the result of addition,
Which often drives golfers to ping-pong and fishin'.

T is for *traps,* and it's downright pathetic
That their pull on one's golf ball should be so **magnetic.**

V is for *virtue,* which golfers possess,
Compared with most men, neither more nor yet less.

W is for *weather,* whose downpouring leak ends
Most often on Monday, the day after week ends.

X is for *Xmas,* when, as a surprise,
A dozen new balls would do better than ties.

Y is for *yell,* which when driving up onto
A green full of players, you'd better do pronto.

Z is for *zero,* the number of times
A poet can work the word "golf" into rhymes.

LATER, PLEASE

On the second tee
It's all right with me
If I start my old topping and botching;
But give me a long one,
A straight one, a strong one,
On the first, when so many are watching.

WORKS BOTH WAYS

When you are learning golf, you're told
   One thing you ought to do
Is go around with one who plays
   A better game than you.

A piece of sound advice, no doubt,
   The only question is,
While you may thus improve *your* game,
   What do you do to *his?*

ESPECIALLY THE CHAIRMAN

Come, shed a tear of honest pity
For members of the Greens Committee,

One time by all, or quite a lot of,
The members of the club well thought of,

Considered friendly, loyal, gentle,
And not too weak in matters mental,

The kind who could be trusted always
To walk behind in darkened hallways,

Quite decent people, liked, respected—
Until, that is, they were elected.

NONE DOWN

First golfer on the moon is he,
Yet mad enough to pop.
Because of lack of gravity,
The poor lad's putt won't drop.

COLD COMFORT

He golfs on coldest days, I've heard,
Alone, with his dog Rover.
For then that water hole, the third,
Thank God, is frozen over!

THE OVER-SWINGER

The over-swinger fails to check
His club, and wraps it round his neck,
And almost hits the ball behind
Before commencing to unwind.

So far his club must travel then,
Before it's at the ball again,
That all the little slips he makes
Are magnified to large mistakes;

And though he swings with might and main,
His effort is, alas, in vain,
Resulting as it does in lots
Of most disreputable shots.

But do not scorn too hastily
The over-swinger, for, you see,
Though not so much as golfing timber,
He is, you must admit, quite limber.

DID KILMER PLAY GOLF?

I think that I shall never see
My ball beneath a spreading tree
Whose roots give me a dreadful lie,
Whose branches strike me in the eye,
Whose leaves obliterate the view,
Whose trunk prevents a follow-through—
I'll never see a tree, I swear,
And not wish it were otherwhere.

DIGGING HIS OWN GRAVE

The divot is a piece of sod
That ought to be replaced and trod
Upon by golfing gentlemen,
And thus allowed to grow again.

For otherwise it leaves a spot
Scooped out and bare, where, like as not,
If there is justice, by and by
The divoteer's own ball will lie.

DON'T ASK ME WHY

Upon the tee I firmly stand,
My trusty driver in my hand,
And just before I take my stance
And start to swing, I cast a glance
Ahead of me. Ah, all is nice,
For I invariably slice,
And to the fairway's right all's clear.
I do not have a thing to fear.
This is, for me, the snap of snaps:
To left, alone, are rough and traps.
And so, without a further look,
I take my stance, and swing—and hook.

THERE ARE FOURS AND FOURS

A screaming drive,
A number five,
A pitch and run,
Then down in one.

A birdie four?
Well, as to score
Quite right you are.
But three is par.

TWO WAYS OUT

Some golfers blast their ball from traps
  With one adroit explosion,
But others, out in ten perhaps,
  Depend upon erosion.

IT MAKES A DIFFERENCE

It's just about four miles around
  The average eighteen,
Where briskly in pursuit I chase
  My ball from tee to green.

I carry all of thirty pounds
  Of clubs and bag and stuff,
And never get too weary or
  Consider it too tough.

But walk from home to office, though
  It's but a fourth as far?
Well, now, that's asking quite a lot,
  I'd better take the car.

LOOK HERE

If only I kept my eye on the ball,
  Looking downward as does the pro there,
I might not see where it was going, at all,
  But there might be a chance it would go there.

GET TOGETHER, PLEASE

The day my dead-eye putts are falling
My drives are at their most appalling,
And when my drives are simply splendid
My putting streak's abruptly ended.

OVER AND OVER

This golfer wears a dunce cap.
He thinks he must, perforce.
For though he isn't stupid,
He does repeat the course.

BAD MOMENT

Heard is the distant, frenzied shout
Of "Fore!" as the ball goes sailing out,
Straight at the head, or another part,
Of some poor innocent, pure of heart,
Who, bent over double, head in hands,
Awaits the moment the stray ball lands,
Hoping the while, though hope is dim,
That the law of averages favors him.

UNKINDEST CUT

This golfer has a wicked slice
And quite a follow-through.
That's why his partner, who stood close,
Is on the green in two.

NO COMPARISON

The fisherman is known to say,
About the one that got away,
That it was a tremendous lot
More lengthy than the one he caught.

The hunter moans about his luck
In coming on a strapping buck,
For shooting perfectly exposed;
The season had, however, closed.

The golfer, though, can talk them stiff
About the score he'd have made if—

FIXING THE BLAME

The tee that's not level,
  The ball that is dead,
The fellow who's talking,
  The slowpokes ahead,

The fairway that's soggy,
  The place of the cup,
The tree needing trimming,
  The wind that came up,

The shaft that is crooked,
  The clubhead that's loose—
It takes little looking
  To find an excuse.

WASTED SKILL

I sank a long and curling putt,
   It's like I've seldom seen;
It would have helped my scoring, but
   'Twas on the practice green.

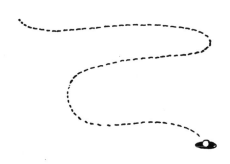

THE MORE FASHIONS CHANGE,
THE MORE GOLF REMAINS THE SAME

Ernie Vossler won the Panama Open in Munsingwear.—*Advertisement.*

We remember, though but dimly,
Those departed days of yore
When we watched great golfers grimly,
Thinking only of their score.

Now we need to know what brogans
Are upon those feet of Hogan's
And just what the slacks are called
That in Memphis or Miami
Drape the shanks of Slammin' Sammy,
Mangrum, Burke, and Finsterwald.

We must know, too, of the sweater
That had Boros playing better
When he gave the crowd a jolt,
And what shirt wore Ken Venturi,
And what watch, in fit of fury,
Took the blows of Tommy Bolt.

Likewise leave us not the riddle
Of what cap donned Cary Middle-
Coff to help him with his game,
And it really would exasperate
If cereal that Casper ate
For breakfast, had no name.

Curiosity we harbor
Re the belt of Jerry Barber
That held up so well his pants,
And it troubles us, some Mondays,
When we can't recall the undies
Littler found improved his stance.

We remember golfers svelteless
When the game they played was all,
But though some were sockless, beltless,
Socked and belted was the ball.

WEEKEND GOLFER

With eighteen holes on Saturday,
  On Sunday, thirty-six,
He goes serenely on his way
  And very seldom kicks.

Five days he works, and two he plays,
  But when he gets to heaven,
Eternally, he hopes and prays,
  He'll get to play all seven.

GENEROSITY

For flattery and kindness what,
   I ask, surpasses this:
Conceding you a two-foot putt
   You probably would miss!

ONE BY ONE

If ever I make a hole-in-one,
  A thrill that I've never known,
I won't be believed and I'll have no fun,
  For I'm sure to be playing alone.

Familiar is the wise,
  All-knowing golfer who'll
At drop of hat apprise
  You of the proper rule,

As, when you've hit the pin,
  Played your opponent's ball,
Been tardy to begin,
  Got rained out by a squall,

Let club rest on the sand
  Or else upon the green,
Brushed gently with your hand
  Some worm cast you have seen.

He knows the rule book well,
  Has read it through and through,
And so can always tell
  What penalizes *you*.

HOME FROM THE RANGE

He's practiced so much on the driving range
  That now, when a golf game calls,
He's the one in the foursome who looks a bit strange
  As he carries a bucket of balls.

GREEN POSTURES

They fidget and fuss
   While behind them we're muttering.
It isn't their putts
   That annoy, it's their puttering.

DOWN PAYMENT

Whenever I'm good,
My opponent is better,
And so, when I bet,
I emerge as the debtor.
Whenever he's bad,
I am always still worse,
And that is why golf's
Such a drain on my purse.

DID I SAY THAT?

Many a golfer gone sour with his hitting
I've heard say, "To hell with the game. I am quitting.
I've played twenty years, and just look at that score!
I'll never, no, never, play any more."

To hear his expressions of anger and sorrow
You never would guess he'd be playing tomorrow.

TEMPER, TEMPER

He's broken 70 at last,
Though still the worst of dubs.
I don't refer to score (don't dast),
I'm speaking of his clubs.

LISTEN TO THIS

The locker room's one
Place at least, where a guy,
When the round is done,
Can improve his lie.

LINES ON LUCK

A golfer's luck is always tough,
   His good luck's simply nil;
The bad bounce goes into the rough,
   The good bounce—hell, that's skill!

SURVEYOR

The one who sights along the green
  To estimate the roll,
And pats and tests the grass between
  Where he is and the hole,

And squats as if about to hatch
  An egg, so slow and boresome,
May sink his putts and win his match
  But lose his happy foursome.

NO HANDICAP

The golfer with the fussy twitch
   Went on to win his match.
It wasn't that he had an itch,
   He merely played at scratch.

HIGH TIME

The sweetest sound that meets the ear,
When trailing slowly in the rear
Of four erratic, dawdling dubs
Who, with their wildly swinging clubs,
Do all the flailing that they do,
Is these four words, "Please play on through."

THE BALL AND THE CURSE
or, LONGFELLOW ON THE LINKS

I hit a ball into the air,
It fell to earth, I knew not where;
For off it flew, sliced to the right,
And suddenly dropped out of sight.

I breathed a curse into the air,
It fell to earth, I knew not where;
For who has sight so keen to see
The flight of words of blasphemy?

Long afterward, behind an oak,
I found the ball. It cost a stroke.
As for the curse, precisely then
I found and breathed it once again.

BIRD IN HAND

On the green there's so much of a flutter
   That the ball isn't easy to hit,
For he putts with a goose-neck putter,
   And the goose doesn't like it a bit.

DECLINE AND FALL

To hit the ball
Upon the level
You have to be
A skillful devil,

But when it's on
A downhill slope,
To skill you add
Both prayer and hope.

ONE DOWN

Weight distributed,
　Free from strain,
Divot replaced,
　Familiar terrain,
Straight left arm,
　Unmoving head—
Here lies the golfer,
　Cold and dead.